Dreams

Learn How To Interpret Your Dreams And Discover The Magic And Beauty Behind Them

Theodore Maddox

© 2015

© Copyright 2015 by Zenith Publishing- All rights reserved.

All rights reserved. No part of this publication may be reproduced, distributed, or transmitted in any form or by any means, including photocopying, recording or other electronic or mechanical methods, without the prior written permission of the author or publisher, except in the case of brief quotations embodied in critical reviews and certain other noncommercial uses permitted by copyright law.

This book is a piece of erotic fiction that contains sexually explicit scenes and adult language. It may be considered offensive to some readers and is not suitable for children. This book is for adults only.

This is a work of fiction. Names, characters, businesses, places, events and incidents are either the products of the author's imagination or used in a fictitious manner. Any resemblance to actual persons, living or dead, or actual events is purely coincidental.

The author recognizes the trademarked status and trademark owners of various products referenced in this work of fiction that have been used without permission. The publication and use of these trademarks is not authorized, associated with or sponsored by the trademark owners.

This eBook is licensed for your personal enjoyment only. This eBook may not be resold or given away to other people. If you would like to share this book with another person, please purchase an additional copy for each recipient. If you are reading this book and did not purchase it, or it was not purchased for your use only, then please return to your favored bookshop and purchase your own copy. Thank you for respecting the hard work of the author.

Table of Contents

Disclaimer / Copyright Info

Introduction

Chapter 1: History of Dream Interpretation

Chapter 2: Remembering your Dreams

Chapter 2: Falling Dreams

Chapter 3: Dreams of being chased

Chapter 4: Dreams of our Teeth Falling Out

Chapter 5: Different Types of Dreams

Conclusion

Introduction

Every night, we go to bed and dream throughout the night weather we remember it or not. Some of our dreams scare us, make us happy, and make us excited and some dreams even wake us up in the middle of the night. When we dream about different topics, we start to often wonder why you dreamt about what we did. Luckily, dreams can be interpreted if you really know what to look for. Most of us dream each night and don't remember our dreams but we often remember those that mean a great deal to us and those that makes us want to identify what the dream meant. Dreams can either mean a great deal to an individual or they may mean nothing at all. Either way, it's important to analyze our dreams as they often have a deeper meaning behind them and they can tell us a great deal about our lives.

If, for example, you're constantly having dreams that you're falling or that your teeth are falling out, there may be a reason behind this that can easily be explained. Dreams will continue to occur regardless of what you feel the meaning is behind them. Some individuals swear by their dreams and feel as though they predict what will happen in their future while others do not think much of their dreams at all. Remember that you are in full control of what your dreams mean to you! Start doing some research and compare your dreams to the different interpretations that you find in order to compare your dreams with the interpretations that you discover.

The primary reason that I have always been fascinated with dreams is because of the tangible effect that dreams can have on mood. Have you ever awoken feeling on edge or depressed, scared or uneasy? Maybe sometimes you open your eyes feeling joyful and inspired, motivated and positive. This is likely due to the dreams you had during the night. Dreams may seem like total works of the imagination, but can they really be considered as such if they're having real impacts on your mood?

Take this for example: I have been skydiving many times in the past and it was a completely exhilarating experience. I felt every emotion from ecstasy to terror and everything in between. Skydiving is a very risky activity and a lot of people are terrified of it because they have a deep fear of heights. There was a time in my life that I had never been skydiving in real life, but only in my dreams. I used to have at least one dream a week about jumping out of a plane and parachuting to safety. In my vivid skydiving dreams, I would have the exact same emotional experience as the ones I had when I actually went skydiving, yet I had never physically jumped out of a plane before. The emotional and mental experiences were the exact same, the only difference was one was a dream and one was physical reality. The point I'm trying to make is that just because dreams lack raw physical experience, they still have a strong psychological impact on us, making them in a sense, real. For what is a memory but merely a recollection of a physical and psychological experience? I would argue that the aspect of memories that makes them, well, memorable, is being able to recall how those memories made you **feel** when they happened.

Dreams are all about feelings that are deeply engrained in our psyches. Some dreams feel as though they are memories of things that have not yet occurred. Have you ever had a dream that you can't remember but you can still **feel** the psychological impact of that dream? Sometimes these dreams cannot only dictate how we feel mentally, but they can also unconsciously impact our physical actions.

I remember once when I was in college I woke up with a few tears in my eyes. I didn't feel sad, in fact, I felt rather inspired and enlightened. I couldn't figure out why I had been crying and I could not for the life of me remember what I had dreamed. I decided to give up trying to remember my dream and I went on with my day. The day went as it usually did, hours of classes and naps in between. When the day was finally done I hopped on the bus and headed for home. I didn't get on the bus that I normally got on though, for some reason I hopped on a bus that took the long way home and made a detour to the local mall. I rarely went to the mall but for some reason I felt compelled to go. Once I arrived, I window-shopped around a feel clothing stores and eventually made my way to a bookstore. College had made me hate reading due to the endless hours of late night textbook reading that I was forced to endure. I had given up on reading for pleasure because every time I did I would feel guilty for not reading my thick psychology textbooks.

I wandered around the bookstore aimlessly but I felt as though I was searching for something. I eventually stumbled upon the sci-fi section and began to browse through some of the books. I picked out three books about space and purchased them with no hesitation at all. I had always been infatuated by space, but this was the first time I had actually purchased a book in years, let alone three! (Not including my pricey college books). I jumped back onto the bus that would take me home and I immediately started reading one of my new books; it was called "Cosmos" by: Carl Sagan. I read the first few pages and then started skimming through the book until I stumbled upon the image section. I searched through the images and then I found it, a beautiful image of the earth taken from the moon. The sight of this image nearly took my breath away, not because of it's elegance, but because it was exactly what I had dreamt about the night before.

Within seconds I was bombarded with an influx of memories from the night before. I could vividly remember every aspect of my dream! I had been on the moon for years, completely alone, wandering through deep valleys searching for an opportunity to gaze upon the earth. One day a gorgeous blonde woman told me I could see the earth from atop the tallest mountain on the moon. I was able to climb up the mountain, but when I finally got there I could see nothing but the blackness of space. I collapsed to the ground, utterly defeated. Then the woman appeared again and told me to turn around. I did as she asked and then I saw the most beautiful sight I could imagine, the earth. I had worked for years to see this view and finally I had achieved my goal. I collapsed to my knees and started weeping in sheer joy.

While this was an amazing dream, it was more amazing to me how the strong memory of this dream had altered my actions the next day. I was a creature of habit and this dream had forced me to act in ways that I usually wouldn't, without me even realizing this. I was in a sense possessed by my dream. This experience really made me wonder how many times this happens to people every single day. Can dreams really have a massive impact on our day-to-day behaviors? I think that they can, which is why I feel that learning to remember and interpret your dreams is very important. In this book I will show you how to do just that. Let's delve into the amazing world of dreams and see what we can discover!

Chapter 1: History of Dream Interpretation

Sigmund Freud, the Father of Psychoanalysis was one of the first individuals to start to analyze dreams and identify what they mean for our lives. The idea of analysis stems from the fact that Freud was fascinated by the fact that the mind was able to reach a high level of activity even without the individual being aware of what exactly was taking place. This fascination lead to investigations being held by Freud and the analysis of dreams and what they mean. Freud believed that our dreams stemmed from an inner wish that we would not admit to and that we repressed. That being said, some of our dreams may be analyzed by this idea but others may not fall under this concept. For example, specific nightmares may not be a wish that is suppressed but is usually something that's taking place that causes us an immense amount of fear. While historical figures like Freud have played a huge role in dream interpretation, dreams have been analyzed for years even before Freud. Throughout history, there has been a constant desire to understand our dreams. We have become incredibly fascinated with dreams and what they mean to our lives. There are an immense amount of books on dreams, individuals who claim to interpret dreams and historical information that will identify what exactly your dreams mean. That being said, it's important to remember that regardless of the information out there, you may find multiple sources with dream interpretation but they may give you different interpretations of your dream.

Throughout history, dreams have been regarded as very important occurrences that need to be evaluated. In Ancient Egypt for example, dreams have been known to be adventures of the soul when the body is asleep. Many different historical groups also believed that dreams are symbols of what's to come in the future and they've also been known to show the path of what an individual should do in a certain situations. Different cultures have different meanings behind dreams and what they are truly describing, but most cultures value dreams and view them as being for important occurrences in our lives that must be analyzed. Dreams throughout history have been known to give us hints of what's to come in the future, they've been known to predict when different diseases and crisis will occur. Dreams have also been known to predict death and sickness. There are many different interpretations of dreams and one will have to analyze their dreams based on their culture and their own personal beliefs. There are tons of interpretations of dreams out there. Many of these interpretations date back hundreds and thousands of years and vary from country to culture.

      Over the years, individual's come up with different interpretations that range anywhere from death predictions to upcoming purchases that should be made. Whatever you dream, ultimately has some type of meaning behind it and it's up to you to identify what your dream means and to what extent does the dream actually apply to your life. Your dreams can range from anything to an upcoming event to something you discussed before you fell asleep. Doing research on different dream interpretations will help you come to your own conclusion regarding what each of your dreams mean and what it says about who you are as an individual. Historically, there are many different ideas and theories behind dreams. Researching many different interpretations will help you identify which interpretation best explains your dreams and the meaning behind each and every one of them. Many of the historical symbols in different dreams have been passed down through different cultures. Many theories have stayed the same while others have changed over the years. Break out an old history book and start doing some research if you want to truly find some meaning behind your dreams. The good news is that there is an immense amount of information regarding dream interpretation that is available for you to read, including this book!

Chapter 2: Remembering your Dreams

We don't always remember our dreams. In fact, if we don't remember our dreams and think about them as soon as we wake up, they will often fade away forever. This inexplicable phenomenon of dream forgetfulness is often thought of as a psychological defense mechanism to protect your mind from harmful thoughts that occur during dreams. If you really want to try and remember all of your dreams, the first thing you want to do is make sure you're getting enough sleep each night. If you're only getting a few hours of sleep each night and you do not know why you can't remember your dreams, it's probably because you're not sleeping enough hours to get your mind at the optimal level to dream. You must be in a deep sleep in order to actually have a complete dream.

Another helpful tip would be to keep a notepad by your bed each night. This dream journal is very important for being able to actually remember all of your dreams. The first thing you want to do is to remember to write down all of your dreams. Now, this means that no matter what you remember, no matter how minor it may seem, you must document this in your dream journal. When you wake up in the morning, before you do anything else, before you stand up, brush your teeth or do anything else, try to remember what your dream was about. You should be writing down your dream right after you open your eyes to ensure that you remember most of your dream. When writing down your dreams it might be helpful to follow these guidelines:

- Who were the characters in your dream?

- What was the location of your dream?

- What was the main issue or event in your dream?

- Did the dream have positive or negative connotations or was it neutral?

- How long did the dream appear to last?

- Have you had the dream before? If so what were the differences and similarities?

- Was the dream lucid? (Did you know you were dreaming?)

- Was the dream viewed from you personal perspective or did you appear to be an observer? (Fly on the wall).

    The more you're able to write down, the more you'll be able to remember over time. Part of the reason why people fail at this is because they start to only write down the important dreams or dreams that they prefer. The more you practice writing down your dreams, the more likely it will be that you continue this process. If you only do this for a few days, you will not give your mind enough time to remember the process of remembering each and every one of your dreams no matter how long or how significant they are. Consistency is key if you really want to remember your dreams!

    If you truly want to try and remember all of your dreams you must write every small fragment down that you can remember. The more that you write down, the more of your dreams you'll be able to remember in the long run. If you wake up at some point during the night and remember the dream you just had, don't go back to sleep feeling confident that you will remember it once your alarm goes off. Write the dream down first and then go back to sleep. Remind yourself when you're falling asleep that you want to wake up and fully remember your dream. We tend to forget our goals when we first wake up in the morning so reminding yourself before you fall asleep will be a helpful tip to help you remember to fill out your dream journal once you wake up. Try reading your dream journal at night before you go to bed. This may encourage and prime you to dream even more and remember more of your dreams as well. You'll start to train your mind to remember what you dreamt about the night before right when you wake up each morning. Keeping your journal close by will be a constant reminder for you to write down your dreams. This is a fun project that can be done at any age level and is often done as Psychology projects while you're in school. Many high school and college psychology teachers will have their students perform this project and turn their journals in after a significant amount of time of running this project.

Keeping a dream journal is important so that you can identify the areas of your life that you may need to work on. You can understand a great deal about what you're facing in your life simply by analyzing your dreams. Now, that being said, many of our dreams are so vivid that we remember immediately when we wake up. For example, some of our dreams feel so real that they may even wake us up in the middle of the night. Some individuals have been woken up by their dream by screaming, crying or even losing their breath. While dreams are often very far from reality when they occur, they often seem very real and we feel as though whatever is happening in our dream is actually happening to us. This feeling can either be a very happy feeling or we may wake up frightened or upset, either way, our dreams can often have a great impact on us. On the other hand, we have dreams that we have to try and piece together when we wake up because they aren't as vivid as other dreams that we may have had. We have different dreams each night for different reasons. Our dreams can be linked to anything from what we were watching before we went to bed, to a conversation that we were having during that day, to something that may be causing us stress and pain throughout our personal or professional life. There are many different reasons behind our dreams but once we start writing down our dreams, the reasoning behind them will become clearer.

When we dream about certain things, we start to wonder why we dreamt what we did. When certain people, animals or other things pop into our dreams, we want to analyze the dream and really figure out why we dreamt about this certain topic. That being said, you will not be able to dream at all if you're sleep deprived. In order to reach an ideal level of sleep where you have vivid dreams, your brain must be relaxed. That being said, if your brain is not as rested as it should be you will not reach the level of REM sleep where you will most likely have lucid dreams. If you're not sleeping enough, you most likely will not dream at all because your brain is not relaxed enough to reach this level of sleep. If you're not dreaming at all, look at your sleep patterns. You may be drinking too much caffeine or staying up too late at night and you're unable to reach an adequate level of sleep that's needed if you truly want to reach a deep sleep where dreams are a possibility. REM sleep or rapid eye movement occurs usually after at least 4-6 hours of sleep and this is when your dreams will become more vivid and you will dream more often.

Most people do not realize this but we actually have multiple dreams each night, we just do not remember all of them. At first, our dreams are very short and only last for a minute or so which is why it's difficult to remember what we dreamt about. Next, once we've been asleep for at least an hour and a half, the second dream will be slightly longer than the first dream. The next two dreams that you have will occur after you've been asleep for about six hours. Once you've been asleep for this significant amount of time, your dreams will be much longer and you will dream anywhere from 45 minutes to a full hour. This is what makes it so important for us to get anywhere from six to eight hours of sleep each night so that we can reach the point of REM sleep and stay in this phase for a significant amount of time. When we are in the phase of REM sleep, this is when we process memories, process information and it's also a therapeutic time as one significant area of REM sleep allows us to deal with any emotional trauma that we may be faced with. While some dreams can be frightening and we want to try and understand why we dream what we do, dreaming is an important part of recovery for our brains. Our brains are incredibly complex and they need a significant amount of time to recover and process new information as well as deal with different things that we may be faced with. Understanding this process is important as you are in charge of how much sleep you get each night. If you are forced to wake up early for work or for other reasons, make sure you try and get to bed at an earlier time in order to give yourself a significant amount of time to recover your brain.

      If you don't believe that dreams are a necessary recovery mechanism for your brain, then try depriving yourself of sleep for a couple days. It has been proven that people who deprive themselves of sleep for long enough will start to hallucinate and dream while they're awake. If that doesn't prove that dreaming is a necessary recovery phase for your brain then I don't know what does. It has even been proven that people who are allowed to sleep, but are woken up right before they enter the dream state, will also begin to hallucinate and dream while there awake, even though they have had some sleep. This shows that it's not just sleeping that's vital to our nightly ritual, but dreaming as well.

Chapter 2: Falling Dreams

One very common dream that many individuals tend to have are falling dreams. On average, most individuals will have multiple dreams about falling within their lifetime. When you dream about falling, you most likely dream about falling to your death, not simply just falling down on the ground or falling down a hill. Your dream is made worse because the dream involves your pending death. These dreams are not only scary due to their vividness, but they can also be quite traumatizing. When we have these dreams, we often wake up sweating or panting from being out of breath. Falling dreams can be very scary as you immediately feel like you do not have any control over a certain situation. For example, you may start to dream of yourself falling off of a building, roof, or a cliff. Some individuals may even dream about falling from an airplane. Many of us believe the myth that if you don't wake up before you fall, you'll die in your sleep. Regardless of the theory behind this myth, the myth is not true, although they are very scary and they feel as though you will if you do not wake up in time.

In order to really understand why we're having these dreams, we have to really search within ourselves to identify what is happening in our personal life that is triggering these falling dreams. If you do not look internally, the problem that is causing the dream to occur will most likely never get resolved and you will continue to have very scary and frightening falling dreams. You may even actually hit the ground in your dream if you do not get to the root of the problem at hand. Falling dreams should not be overlooked and they most definitely should be investigated.

When you start to dream about falling you begin to feel like you have no control. You start to feel as though you're falling in your dream and you have nothing that will prevent you from falling. This is not only a scary feeling but you start to feel as though you're going to permanently lose control. These dreams can often occur because of something in your personal life. Something may be happening in your personal or professional life that is making you feel like you're losing control which would then lead to a falling dream.

When we're faced with issues at work for example, that are out of our control, it can be very frustrating for us. Maybe there was a project or another employee that was creating a situation that you have no control over and this is frustrating and upsetting for you, it may result to a nightmare or a falling dream. When you feel out of control, this thought is in your mind and even though you may not realize that you're thinking about it, it very well might be consuming your daily thoughts and your nightly dreams. Another area of your life may be your personal life where you feel like you are losing control. We often enter into relationships and they do not work out as planned. When our relationship with our significant other gets to a point where we feel like we have no control over it, we tend to become very overwhelmed by this thought. While many of us do not like to always be in control of situations, most of us do however want to be in charge of our own lives and whatever happens to us each day. If something is happening to us and we do not feel strong enough to remove ourselves from the situation, we will feel trapped and stuck in a situation. When we feel trapped, we feel as though there's no way out and we start to feel like we will never get to a place where we can remove ourselves, which in turn leads to negative thoughts. These negative out of control thoughts often lead to our falling dreams. A falling dream almost always coincides with a situation in your waking life where you're feeling out of control.

Falling dreams can be linked to feeling out of control over a certain situation or over your entire life, but it can also be related to insecurities. When you dream that you're falling, one interpretation suggests that you have this dream when you lack confidence within yourself. When you are insecure, you feel as though you're not adequate and not good enough. This is a possible reason for the falling dreams that you may be experiencing. When you feel like you're falling, you're feeling unstable and out of control which may be caused by what you feel on a daily basis. For example, if you feel insecure and unstable as an individual, this may lead to dreams of falling. Insecurities can affect us in many different ways. They are scary feelings that make us feel out of control and inadequate, when we're feeling this way it not only disrupts our daily lives, but it interferes with our sleep cycle as well. That being said, these feelings of insecurity may not just be due to personal reasons. Yes, you may feel insecure about yourself and what you look like, which in turn may cause the dreams of falling but insecurities in other areas of your life may also lead to frightening falling dreams. For example, if you're at risk of losing your job or your home you may feel insecure about those areas of your life and it will make you have a dream about falling. Also, if you feel insecure in your relationship and you feel as though you may lose your significant other, this will also create vulnerable feelings and low self-esteem, which will then lead to falling nightmares. If new demands such as in the workplace or in a relationship in your life have now been placed on you, this may also lead to falling dreams. Falling dreams can be very scary and it's important to get to the bottom of why these dreams are occurring. What are you being faced with in your life that's either making you feel insecure or out of control in your life? Whatever it is, once you identify the problem you should be able to eliminate these nightmares from your life.

Chapter 3: Dreams of being chased

Dreams of being chased by someone or something is very common. When we dream about being chased, it's often a very terrifying experience. We find ourselves running as fast as we can but we are unable to escape whatever is chasing us. This can be incredibly terrifying. Oftentimes, when we have this dream, we are unable to scream and no matter how hard we try nothing comes out. We may even dream about trying to run away but our legs won't move and there's no way to get away. Something or someone is coming after you and as much as you want to scream for help or get up and run away, you can't because you've lost your voice and your legs won't allow you to move and run away. This can be a very frustrating and scary experience. There's something coming after you and there's nothing you can do about it. When we have these dreams, we often start to wonder why they occurred. There are many different interpretations for these types of dreams.

One interpretation of a chasing dream is a possible feeling of being victimized. If you're feeling like you're being chased, in reality, you may feel like someone is victimizing you. This may include being victimized by another individual, a coworker, a significant other or possibly even a family member. When you feel victimized you feel bullied and you feel like the person who is victimizing you has control over you, which is a very scary thought to have. No one wants to feel victimized and we may not even realize that what we're feeling is serious until these thoughts start to consume our dreams. Once we realize that these dreams are occurring, it's important to look into the problem. Find out who you're feeling victimized by and identify a solution for the problem. Do not let these dreams and these feelings go unnoticed. Once you are able to link your dreams with something that is actually occurring in your real life, you want to handle the situation immediately. That being said, when you're feeling victimized, you may not feel victimized by one person only, you may be feeling victimized by society as a whole. When you're feeling this way, like society is out to get you and like nothing ever goes your way, you want to find ways to deal with these problems and issues in your daily life to ensure that they do not interrupt your sleep cycle each night. As discussed earlier, it is very common for us to not even realize that different things that are happening in our lives or that certain things are even a problem until we start to have these dreams and they force us to look into what's happening in our real life to make these dreams occur.

What are we running from? If we identify the fact that we're not feeling victimized by anyone or anything, we must then look at what else is happening in our life that's making us run. Are we running from a relationship? Are we running from a person? Maybe we're even running from a job or career choice. We may feel like society is against us in some way and that is why we're running as fast as we can to get away from a situation at hand. For example, maybe we are feeling stuck in a relationship with someone who wants to get married. Well, if we're not ready for this type of commitment, or if we're not ready to be in this type of relationship with someone, we may feel trapped and overwhelmed, which in turn would lead to a dream about being chased by someone or something. When this happens, we're not necessarily running away from the person in our dream but possibly just the entire situation. The same type of situation may occur if we're feeling unhappy with our job or career choice. We may feel stuck in whatever position we're in and we start to dream about running away from our job and running towards something better. Either way, when you have a dream about being chased, it's important to analyze the situation in your real life to make sure you're not feeling victimized in your life and to make sure you're not feeling stuck in a particular situation in your life.

It's very common for children to have dreams of being chased due to the immense amount of bullying that is taking place in schools today. Children are having these nightmares and running into their parents' room for help. When a situation like this occurs with a child, it's important for the parent to ask the child what is happening at school to identify why they are having these dreams. One of the common signs of bullying in children is nightmares and sleep disturbances. If this happens, parents need to get to the root of the problem to ensure that their child is not being bullied at school. When a child is feeling helpless, he/she will often have a dream about being chased and it may be linked to bullying, or something else they are being faced with in their life to make them feel as though they have no control and they are feeling hopeless about whatever they are experiencing in their daily lives.

Another reason we may have a dream of being chased is when we're trying to escape our responsibilities. When different things happen in our lives, we tend to often become very overwhelmed. For example, if you're in a relationship and you've just discovered that you're going to be a parent, this may be a very scary experience. Immediately, we may think to ourselves that we want to get ourselves out of the situation simply out of fear. When we're faced with challenged, our immediate thought may be to run away and escape these changes. We don't want to grow up and many individuals are afraid of change. Change can be intimidating and often very scary, which can lead to dreams of being chased. When these feelings are linked with our dreams of being chased it's safe to say that it's most likely due to the fact that we're trying to run away from our responsibilities. Even though we may not actually be running away in our real life, we may be running away in our dreams because we're subconsciously thinking about running away from reality due to fear and intimidation.

    Another example would be if you were give a promotion at work and you are feeling overwhelmed by the amount of work that you not have in front of you. This thought alone of feeling fearful and feeling more like an adult due to an immense amount of responsibilities may lead to a dream of being chased because you start to feel as though life is chasing you and forcing you to grow up and be an adult when you're not fully ready and able to. Ultimately, dreams of being chased and running away are often a result of feeling fearful or overwhelmed by a certain situation. We often resort to running away from situations rather than dealing with them and this in turn leads to the frightening dreams of being chased by a serial killer, monster, an animal, or possibly a large group of people. Whatever the reason is for the dreams of being chases, you must identify what and who you are actually trying to run away from in your life so that you can identify what your plan of action needs to be to ensure that you don't actually run away from individuals or different situations in your real life, unless it proves necessary. Identify what you're feeling fearful of and what you're trying to get away from. Identify what it is in your life that you are trying to avoid so that you can fix the problem. Do not continue to run away from things in life. Face the problem head on so that you can eliminate these nightmares.

Chapter 4: Dreams of our Teeth Falling Out

Our teeth are some our most prized possessions. We value our teeth for many reasons. For one, our teeth help us nourish our bodies and chew our food and the other reason is that they help us smile. As individuals, our appearance means a great deal to us and we do not want to have something wrong with our mouth that makes us look different from others. Yes, we all have differences but we do not want to show others that we do not have teeth as this is a sign of lack of care and malnourishment. That being said, if we dream that we are losing our teeth it can be an incredibly scary experience as our teeth will not grow back. If we lose our teeth, we would have to either buy new fake teeth or leave our mouth as is, which would definitely not be recommended. This recurring dream can be frightening and there are a few reasons that may lead to us having this type of dream. This specific dream can often occur as a result of some type of transition taking place in your life.

We're all faced with different types of transitions in our lives. We transition between jobs, partners, and we even transition to different living spaces. These transitions can often be scary for us because they involve change and most of us do not like change. Change can be something that is difficult to adjust to and we may even be fearful of changes such as moving and entering into a new relationship but change can be a good thing for us! That being said, when we're faced with different transitions and it creates a sense of fear within us, we often have dreams of losing our teeth. When these dreams occur, they often represent the fear and anxiety we feel when we are faced with these transitions. The feeling of thinking we are losing our teeth represents that same kind of fear that we think about when we think about the change, loss or transition taking place in our life. Dreams of losing our teeth can occur at any point in our life but they commonly occur in children when they are moving out of childhood and into adulthood which is obviously a huge transition in life. Also, many women have experienced dreams of having their teeth fall out when they are going through menopause as this also represents a huge change in a woman's life.

Along with transitions in your life, we may dream about losing our teeth when we are insecure. Many of us have insecurities; in fact, it wouldn't be normal if you, as an individual did not have an insecurity about something in your life. That being said however, there are many individuals whose insecurities truly take over their life and become very unhealthy. When an individual is insecure to a level that it interrupts their daily life, they may have dreams about losing their teeth. Specifically, if you're concerned about your image and how others see you, you may have this dream. This dream is common in individuals who are suffering from insecurities because they are constantly thinking about their appearance. When we're feeling insecure about how we look, we may be very self-conscious and this thought may enter our dreams. Insecurities about how we look can impact our inner thoughts, as we tend to not feel good enough when we're insecure. When we do not feel like we look good enough to keep up with society this in turn creates a great deal of other problems in our lives. When we feel this way within ourselves, it may provoke a bad dream of losing our teeth to occur. If we were to lose our teeth it would change our appearance, which is a great fear to those with an already enormous amount of physical insecurities.

When we lose our teeth as a child, we are often made fun of even if it is done in a lighthearted way. Specifically, when we lose our front teeth, this can be a very awkward time for any child, not to mention a time where it is difficult to eat! When we are made fun of or when jokes are made about us losing our teeth, these memories stick with us and often make whatever insecurities we are facing even worse as these thoughts stick in our mind. This old memory of being made fun of when our teeth fall out can encourage a nightmare of a similar situation. During our dream, we go back to our childhood and relive the anxiety and fear of losing our teeth, but it's even worse in our dream because we are now adults and it's not normal for your teeth to fall out as an adult. Especially since they will not grow back! If you've been made fun of or you're in a position in your life where you feel inadequate, you may have a dream of losing your teeth as well.

Another reason that we may lose our teeth in our dreams is due to the fact that we've lost something in our real life. This can be anything from an item to an actual person. If we've lost something that means a great deal to us, this loss may roll over to our dream and we may then have a dream that we're losing our teeth just as we have lost something in our life when we're awake. If you're aware of the fact that you lost something or someone recently, you may be able to link this loss with the loss of your teeth in your nightmare. Another dream that you may have is a dream about losing your teeth and then seeing false teeth in your dream. If this is something that happens in your dream, it may be happening because you are having fears of getting older which is why the false teeth would be present. You may have other dreams that are due the fears that you may be having about getting older but the dreams about false teeth are in fact very common when you're fearful of aging and getting older in life. We are all fearful of getting older but we must learn how to deal with these feelings and channel them appropriately instead of letting these feelings consume our lives to a level where we are dreaming about these fears and letting them consume our dreams. Do not let fears of getting older consume your life and take over your dreams. If you've just hit a milestone age, embrace this time and think of yourself as getting wiser not older. Keep a positive mindset and your nightmares about getting older will slowly fade away. Enjoy the time you have left, don't dwell on the time that's past!

Chapter 5: Different Types of Dreams

While it may seem like all dreams are the same, they are not. There are many different types of dreams that you may have each night. Dreams fall under different classifications based on what exactly happens in your dream. For example, the first type of dream that you may have are psychological healing dreams. These dreams can be some of the most frightening because they are often dreams about something that has actually occurred in your life and that may have caused you pain or hardships. These dreams may be events that have taken place in the past or they may be dreams that involve hardships that you're facing on a daily basis. Psychological healing dreams often occur when you're under a great deal of stress. For example, if something is bothering you at work and you're having trouble dealing with it, you may have disturbing dreams about whatever is bothering you. These dreams often occur to help you overcome whatever obstacle you're facing in your life.

Another type of dream that you may have is a belief dream. These dreams are often based around religious beliefs. When you have belief dreams, they are often related directly to whatever you believe as far as your religion goes. Dreams are often related to the bible and biblical individuals. Problem-solving dreams are also very common. These dreams are incredibly helpful for the dreamer as they work to solve any problem that you may be faced with. Your mind continues to function and think even when you're sleeping. These dreams are helping you think of ways to solve problems in your life by analyzing the situation to identify the best possible outcome. Often times, when individuals have problem-solving dreams, they wake up knowing how to solve a problem that they have been faced with. These problems can range from anything in your personal to professional life. If we were able to choose our dreams, most of us would most likely choose problem-solving dreams as they help us through obstacles we're facing!

Physiological dreams are also very common. These specific dreams are directly linked to our own needs as individuals when we're conscious. For example, if you're dreaming that you're sitting directly in the sun and sweating, this may mean that you need to simply remove a blanket that you have over you. Or you may have a dream that you need to use the restroom and when you wake up, sure enough, you have to go! Whatever you're body needs, you will often have dreams about these needs. Other dreams that we have may simply be about our daily life. Remember that not all of our dreams have to be symbolic and they don't have to have a hidden meaning behind them. Sometimes we simply dream about people that we see every day and people that affect our lives. Every day we tend to do similar things. We go to work, we exercise, we socialize with our friends and these every day occurrences often pop up in our dreams and do not necessarily mean anything, they are just reflections of what we do on a daily basis. For example, if you're a receptionist, you may have dreams about answering phones or filing paperwork.

Compensatory dreams may also occur and they show the other side of our personality that we choose to not reveal to others. We may have hidden desires that we do not carry out in our daily life that would lead us to have compensatory dreams. For example, if you're someone who always follows the rules, you may dream about breaking the rules or doing something that you shouldn't be doing. These dreams allow us to do things that we normally would not do in our daily lives. We all have hidden wants and needs that we do not follow through with. These dreams allow us to follow through with them without letting it affect our normal conscious life. Lucid dreams are also very common and they are also very popular as far as research goes. When a dreamer has a lucid dream, they are aware that they are dreaming but the dream feels so real that the dreamer feels as though it's actually happening to them even though they know that they're not awake. Everything that happens is exaggerated in lucid dreams and when an individual wakes up they often want to research these dreams due to the fact that they felt so real. That being said, lucid dreams do not necessary have a symbolic meaning behind them.

Another type of dream that we have are psychic dreams. These are dreams that occur at night for the dreamer but later on when they're awake the dream actually takes place, which would make the dreamer to be somewhat of a psychic as they somehow were able to predict what would happen to them in the near future. Basically, if something occurs in your life that you dreamt about at some point, it's considered to be a psychic dream. It's a sign of the future. Keep in mind however that a psychic dream is very different than a premonition. A premonition does not necessarily occur when an individual is asleep like a dream does. Some individuals believe in these psychic dreams while others do not. Remember that what you believe your dreams to mean, ultimately describe your own personal belief system.

When we dream, we often find ourselves having recurring dreams. When this happens, it simply means that we need to take a deeper look at the recurring dream that we're having. Whatever we're dreaming about is not being addressed. With each dream that we have, there is often a message that most likely applies to our life. If we are not paying attention to this message, we will continue to have the same dream until we see the message and do something about it. If we keep dreaming about fixing a relationship with someone who we may not be on good terms with, this may mean that we need to make a phone call in order to mend the relationship. When someone is bothering us, we'll also continue to dream about whatever the issue is as well. If the problem is not solved, we will continue to dream about the issue until it is resolved. Lastly, the final type of dream that we may have is a nightmare. Nightmares are the most terrifying dreams that take place. Often times, our nightmares represent things that are taking place in our daily life. Nightmares are incredibly draining and terrifying when they are experienced. Not only are dreams scary but they're draining because we often wake up in a cold sweat, shaking, or screaming which can often take a lot of energy out of us. When our entire body reacts to a nightmare, the severity of the nightmare is often very high. Nightmares are unpleasant and are heightened emotional responses to either people or situations that are taking place within our dreams. Some individuals have a lot of nightmares and are often afraid to fall asleep because of the nightmares they are facing.

Nightmares can take various forms. Often times they can be regular dreams but sometimes they will show up as night terrors or sleep paralysis. Night terrors occur when you suddenly awake, often in a terrified state in which you are yelling or crying. These terrors can be very traumatic but are usually considered less intense than sleep paralysis. Sleep paralysis occurs when you are either falling asleep or waking up. Essentially you become caught in a world between wakefulness and sleep. People who experience sleep paralysis often report not being able to move or speak; they feel as though their minds are perfectly awake while their bodies remain asleep. This may not sound that scary, but as a person who has experienced sleep paralysis I can tell you that it is one of the scariest things I've ever experienced.

If you find yourself having many nightmares, you must get to the root of this problem in order to eliminate the nightmares from your life. Nightmares are terrifying and can leave a lasting impact on our lives. We often have nightmares that we remember throughout our entire lives, due to the impact they've had on us. Nightmares can occur when we're under a great deal of stress, when we've lost someone in our life, when we're sick or they can occur for no reason at all. If they are recurring, this is something that you should look into. We often become so consumed with work, and individuals in our lives that cause us stress or pain that we are unable to turn these thoughts off. When we can't turn the thoughts off, they often roll over into our dreams and affect our sleep cycle as well as our normal life. Most nightmares are fairly normal. Most individuals will have a great deal of nightmares throughout their life. That being said, if your nightmares reach a level where they're causing you a ton of anxiety when you're awake and they are affecting your waking life, there is probably a deeper issue related to this that should be evaluated. Nightmares can be linked to different disorders, diseases and even medications. If you find yourself having multiple nightmares, discuss this with your doctor. He/she may need to change a certain type of medication that you're on or he/she may prescribe you something else that will help you sleep throughout the night. Other doctors may suggest that you try meditation and yoga in order to find inner peace within yourself and eliminate the frightening nightmares from your life all together.

Conclusion

While it's important to understand that there are many common themes related to dreams, a true dream interpretation will be your own interpretation of what your dream means to you. You can spend your time looking up your dreams and reading books about dream interpretations but you are the only one that can truly pull apart your dream and identify the reasoning behind each dream that you may be having. While some dreams are very common and often occur for many of us such as dreams of falling and being chases, each one of us will have a different reason for having this specific dream. These dreams are unique to our lives and to our personal situations. We do not all dream the same way and what one dream means for one person may not be the same for another individual. One individual may have a dream about being chases because they are feeling overwhelmed with a new job and another individual may have a dream about being chased because they have a baby on the way which in turn leads to new responsibilities. Each of us may have the same dream for different reasons and it's important to remember this. Many cultures and individuals have different definitions for what dreams mean and you must remember that whatever you dream can only truly be analyzed by you because you are the only one that truly knows what's happening in your life that may have caused the dream to occur.

While it's important to pay attention to your dreams and learn from them, do not be so consumed with everything that you dream that you feel even more anxious and more pressure. If you dream that you're falling, this does not necessarily mean that something bad is going to happen in your life. If you have a dream that you're pregnant, this does not mean that you're actually pregnant in your real life and it does not necessarily mean that you will become pregnant anytime soon. Remember that what we watch before we fall asleep at night and what we discuss with others may affect our dreams as well. If we have a discussion about a serial killer before we go to bed, this same serial killer or one like him may very well pop up in our dream that night. What we think about and what we discuss often enters into our thoughts at night as well. Pay attention to your dreams. Your dreams may be whatever is on your mind but they may also be a deeper issue that you need to identify in your life in order to eliminate the bad dreams from occurring. Research your dreams if you'd like but do not be consumed by your dreams. Whatever you dream will not necessarily happen in your life and you do not have to follow everything that happens in your dream to have a truly happy life. Take all of your dreams with a grain of salt and make your dream research a fun experience rather than an overwhelming one!

BONUS SAMPLE:

GET SMARTER

30 Ways to Change the Way People perceive You, Increase Your Intelligence and Become the Greatest Version of Yourself

Theodore Maddox

© 2015

© Copyright 2015 by Zenith Publishing- All rights reserved.

All rights reserved. No part of this publication may be reproduced, distributed, or transmitted in any form or by any means, including photocopying, recording or other electronic or mechanical methods, without the prior written permission of the author or publisher, except in the case of brief quotations embodied in critical reviews and certain other noncommercial uses permitted by copyright law.

This book is a piece of erotic fiction that contains sexually explicit scenes and adult language. It may be considered offensive to some readers and is not suitable for children. This book is for adults only.

This is a work of fiction. Names, characters, businesses, places, events and incidents are either the products of the author's imagination or used in a fictitious manner. Any resemblance to actual persons, living or dead, or actual events is purely coincidental.

The author recognizes the trademarked status and trademark owners of various products referenced in this work of fiction that have been used without permission. The publication and use of these trademarks is not authorized, associated with or sponsored by the trademark owners.

This eBook is licensed for your personal enjoyment only. This eBook may not be resold or given away to other people. If you would like to share this book with another person, please purchase an additional copy for each recipient. If you are reading this book and did not purchase it, or it was not purchased for your use only, then please return to your favored bookshop and purchase your own copy. Thank you for respecting the hard work of the author.

Foreword By: Buck Langesley.

Congratulations on downloading this Ebook. My name is Buck Langsley and I met Theodore Maddox about 15 years ago, on a plane headed to New Mexico. Theo sparked up a conversation with me by asking me if I had ever thought about skydiving. I told him I had not. We talked for the entire plane ride and by the end of it I considered Theo a great new friend. He had given me his email address and we soon began having conversations online. We were both living in New Brunswick at the time and Theo eventually convinced me to go skydiving with him. It was an amazing experience and one that I will never forget.

    I have never met somebody as adventurous and eager to learn as Theodore Maddox. The man never stops moving and I'm convinced he's going to live to be over 100 years old. When he told me he was writing this book I told him he's an arrogant bastard. I was just kidding around with him but he still proceeded to ensure me that he was not writing the book to stroke his ego. He wasn't lying and he truly does want to help people, just like he does every day at his psychology clinic. He would never admit it, but Theo is extremely intelligent and full of wisdom. His motivation is extremely inspiring and he has helped me through many trials and tribulations in my own life. I'm very happy that he wrote this book, as I'm sure it will help anybody that it reaches. Being smart is a noble thing to seek and with the help of Theodore anybody can heighten his or her general intelligence. I'm sure you will gain a lot of insight from this book, just as I did.

    Theodore has even inspired me to start writing books myself and I feel as though I've finally found my true passion. I hope you enjoy this book as much as I did, keep in mind as you read that if you knew Theodore as well as I do, you would realize that he is not trying to be condescending in any way. He only wants to keep things simple so that every one of his readers can follow along and benefit from what he knows. Prepare to get smarter, enjoy!

Table of Contents

Intro………..Paul's Big Question & One Wild Ride in Rio

Chapter 1…Dialogue & Common Grammatical Mistakes

Chapter 2…Question Everything, But Don't Overdo It

Chapter 3……Remember, Remember. Use it or Lose it

Chapter 4……Passion = Knowledge

Chapter 5……Look the Part

Chapter 6……Stay Current

Conclusion……Paul's Big Answer

Printed in Great Britain
by Amazon.co.uk, Ltd.,
Marston Gate.